Other books by Steven Bates

Reflections of a Beret

The 'After' Life

Beyond the 'After' Life

More Life to Live

With poetry selections in the following:

Calueche Chronicles by Josh Walker

Forgotten Places by Josh Walker

Acknowledgements

This being a culmination of four previous books compiling strictly poems that deal with PTSD, depression, suicidal thoughts as well as hope and faith, I could not in good faith proceed without acknowledging everyone mentioned in the previous books. That being said, I also shouldn't bore the reader with a long laundry list of people they have never heard of, will never know, will never meet, nor probably will not give a second thought to after reading this acknowledgment. This book is about you the reader however, so it is you whom I acknowledge most. It is because of you this book is written, published, and freely distributed thru the non-profit PoemSpeak.org . It is because of you that I care enough to write these poems, to put into words what I and others have experienced in our struggles with PTSD, depression and suicidal thoughts and attempts. It is my hope that you the reader understand that you are not alone, that you can survive what you are experiencing, and that you are loved and cared for by not only persons that know you in your life but by me and your Creator as well. It is you to whom I need and want to say:

I care about you, I value you, I acknowledge you.

So please,

Stay safe,

Stay strong,

And by all means possible,

Stay Alive!

For distribution through

www.PoemSpeak.org

For anyone struggling with PTSD, depression, or suicidal thoughts

For those caring for loved ones

For those trying to understand

Dedicated

To

My Mother

Janet C Bates

1944-2021

RIP

Sanctified now Glorified

Stay Safe, Stay Strong, Stay Alive

By Steven W Bates

Table of Contents

PTSD

INVISIBLE WOUNDS

From waking in the dead of night,

With nightmares filled with endless fright

From Sweating in a crowded room,

With morbid thoughts of pending doom

From terrifying thoughts and dreams

That fill our minds with endless screams

From pressure felt in chest and head

With feeling of impending dread

From fears unjustified to those

Whom never faced such deadly foes

From such dark places, our fear it flows

With anger matched, Heaven only knows

The hardship of living, day by day it grows

But from all of this we will still strive to be

What we were before crossing over the sea

Please understand it's not the life that we chose

To have fear hang upon us like old, tattered clothes

To have shackled to us the pain and grief

And yet forever hoping to find some relief

From our hearts to yours, may you please understand

This wasn't our dream, this life wasn't planned

Though our visible scars may show the war we've been in

It's our invisible wounds that cut deepest within

Thoughts and Reflections

COMMON THREAD OF PTSD

It's not always bullets nor bombs bursting in air

It's not always shrapnel whizzing fast by your ear

It's not always the sounds of guns and grenades

It's not always the feeling of death coming in spades

It's not always the mortars, RPGs, IEDs,

It's not always but it could be just some of these

It could also be events that were out of control

And if you were the victim from which it has taken its toll

It could also be trauma that was too much to bear

And you suffered greatly from the worst kind of scare

Whatever the causes and whatever the reasons

I'm here for you always, a friend for all seasons

I've had my own kinds of trauma and my own little hell

And I suffer as you do, and others suffer as well

Our traumas have made us become what we are

As silent we fight what has no visible scar

Together we'll press on thought, we'll stand the good fight

Our hands intertwined, they'll soon know our might

We'll work with each other with one common thread

Till the memories we're fighting are tamed in our head

We'll stand with each other and be there as friends

Till the nightmares inside us finally come to an end

Thoughts and Reflections

_____
_____
_____
_____
_____
_____
_____
_____
_____
_____
_____
_____
_____
_____
_____
_____
_____
_____
_____
_____
_____
_____
_____
_____
_____
_____
_____
_____
_____
_____
_____
_____
_____
_____
_____
_____
_____

FLASHBACKS

Memories merging

    Into one

Nightmares purging

    All the fun

Sacred prayers are said

    In Vain

As Haunted Eyes relive

    The Pain

As Sadness, Grief, and endless Horror

Flash silently in dreams abhorred

Then cries of anguish, doom, despair

Escape from lips into the air

As simple sounds disturb the night

Startling them with unknown fright

Dawn brings the sun, a fresh new day

Yet weary eyes can't look away

And ears can't deafen to the sounds

Of piercing tones from whistling rounds

Then smells return to fool the mind

Of another place, another time

The burden's heavy and takes its toll

To traumas burned within the soul

And as pain refreshes and hope may fall

The scars may never show ...at all

Thoughts and Reflections

QUESTIONS

Have you killed anyone?

Have you fired your gun?

Have you shot or been wounded?

Did you do it for fun?

Did you stab anyone

With your bayonet sharp?

Have you looked in one's eyes

As they faded to dark?

Have you suffered enough

From these questions they ask

Have you suffered them quietly

Or taken the asker to task?

Have you just let them know

That it just isn't right

Have you explained that their questions

Bring you right back into the fight?

Have you stood there so silent

While the pain flows again

And the questions keep firing

Like the wind driven rain?

(cont.)

Thoughts and Reflections

(cont..)

To those who don't understand

It's so hard to explain

The wounds cutting deeper

The grief and the pain

So next time they ask

For what they think they should know

Explain in short phrases

Take a breath, deep and slow

Tell them their knowledge

That they seek to gain

Is not worth the heartache

It's not worth the pain

For the memories you have

Are not meant to be shared

And they shouldn't ask

For answers they're not prepared

For though the burden is heavy

And their answers never known

You carry it for them

It's something you bear alone

Thoughts and Reflections

MY DREAMS AND I

Alone at last, my dreams and I

Till nightmares overtake us

Strong we are, unafraid to die

Till flashbacks try to break us

I close my eyes and try to breathe

So pleasant dreams return here

But memories, like eels they seethe

And creep in my mind with fear

The shadows on the wall take form

Like frightening ghosts and things

That swirl around as if a storm

With all the fear that brings

The whispers on the wind set sail

Like demon sounds surrounding

In voices haunting, old and frail,

With heartbeats loud and pounding

I tell myself it's in my mind

These tortuous scenes and phrases

Repeating mantras soft and kind

Till peace, it's head it raises

Then comes the nightmares once again

And my mind remains their evil playpen

Thoughts and Reflections

PTSD

We live medicated

"Mental cases" we're called

For our wrath has hurt loved ones

And they, our actions appalled

To them, we're a stranger

Someone they never knew

For exposed once to danger,

O'er the cuckoo's nest we flew

We fly into rages

And sink into lows

And take ourselves places

That only Heaven knows

But to those that were wounded

Lost and eye, leg, or arm

Refuse to acknowledge us

Since there's no sign of harm

But I say to those wounded

Whom I hold honor and respect

They are the lucky ones

Their wounds fund no neglect

(cont)

Thoughts and Reflections

They have something to show

For the sympathy vote

And look down on us

With a sneer and a gloat

I would rather have crutches

Or be wheelchair bound

Than live with this affliction

Only my mind carries 'round.

Thoughts and Reflections

JUSTIFY ME

Give me a crutch

Give me a cane

Just give me something

That shows for the pain

Give me a wound

Give me a scar

Just give me something

People can see from afar

To show that I'm wounded

To show I'm in pain

To show that I'm not

Having it all in my brain

My wounds, they run deeply

Bu no-one can see

So please give me something

To justify me

Please give me something…. to justify me….

Thoughts and Reflections

TRIALS AND TRIED

From sweaty jungles and gritty sands

To stinking trenches in far off lands

From tunnels built for smallest man

To shrapnel skies in a flying can

Fighters. Soldiers, Sailors all

Have stood for us when heard the call

Some paid the price that war demands

Or made down payments with legs and hands

With determined chin they try to heal

But no one told then just how to feel

When coming home to peace and love

And to never fearing the skies above

To never need check behind each door

Or take a dive and hit the floor

When sounds so common to you and me

Fill that same vet with anxiety

That creaking floor, that coffeepot dripping

Could slowly start his façade to slipping

What once was calm and loving man

May have changed in him what he can't understand

(cont)

Thoughts and Reflections

(cont.)

And without more help, understanding and grace....

That saddened troop may have to face

A jury of 12 that have no clue

Of what PTSD and war can do to you

They'll convict without hearing all of the facts

And call him a "Rambo" because of his acts

The 12 would forget he would have laid down his life

For every one's mother, brother, sister, and wife ...

They'll sit on the court benches dictating his end

Till the gavel hammers in the final judgment to rend

And the life of a hero is cut short once again

But not from the actions in wars he's been in

You see, WAR called the shots, and it knew it would win

To a troop whose coming home was his only real sin.

Thoughts and Reflections

SCARS

Surgery scars, I have a few

Scars from youthful antics too

Scars that show my wilder side

Scars with shame I try and hide

But the deepest scars no one can see

Are the scars that dwell inside of me

The wounds though old, still hurt me so

As the painful feelings from them flow

As they reopen every night

They fill my mind through eyes shut tight

With Fear like blood seeping through the scabs

Though deep inside, their pain it stabs

It haunts me, taunts me, till my minds it screams

As these scars remember most traumatic scenes

Though through vivid dreams and waking scares

The scares aren't seen, so no one cares

But though none can see these scars inside

They're a part of me that can't be denied

Their pain, their hurt, will never heal

Like oozing wounds that never seal

And though I pray I'll not succumb

These scars define who I've become

And though my life's not what I planned

Scarred and wounded, here I stand!

Thoughts and Reflections

INSIDE MY MIND

Inside my mind, my thoughts run free

In battles no one else can see

In fighting for a cause that's right

With demons taunting through the night

Throughout the day that fear remains

Though hidden, it prevails and reigns

It makes me look behind each door

Always searching, forever more

Forever fearing that my old foe

Hides wherever shadows grow

My scars and demons, though none can see

Are with my mind, and still run free

Thoughts and Reflections

FIVE SENSES OF A VETERAN AND FIRST RESPONDER

I've seen things no man should see

And heard the screams that haunted me

I've tasted death with the Kiss of Life

And touched the pulse of the Afterlife

I've smelled the stench of the slipped away

And cried when Death has claimed its prey

I've served in ways I can't describe

For fear of rambling in diatribe

I've survived it all and lived to tell

What Life is like in Earthly Hell

And though my dreams still show the strain

I'd live it all, each day of pain

I'd fight the evil, the sick, depraved

To know just once, a life, I saved.

Thoughts and Reflections

LIVING WITH PTSD

Therapy and psychotropic drugs

Inner peace and embracing hugs

Introspection, sharing pain

Methods all to train the brain

Methods tried and methods failed

Methods yet to have success prevail

For helping us to find a way

To live like normal day to day

To make us "fit" in society

Without our life as the enemy

Perhaps someday a method will work

And from our Life we will not shirk

But till that day of success we see

We'll struggle through living with PTSD

Thoughts and Reflections

_____
_____
_____
_____
_____
_____
_____
_____
_____
_____
_____
_____
_____
_____
_____
_____
_____
_____
_____
_____
_____
_____
_____
_____
_____
_____
_____
_____
_____
_____
_____
_____
_____
_____
_____
_____
_____
_____
_____
_____
_____

8th FLOOR

(Written while receiving care in the 8th floor OKC VA Mental Ward)

The moans, the groans

The cries of pain

The fears of loss

And nothing to gain

The tears of sorrow

Anguish and grief

Pure anger and rage

Without any relief

Anxious and sweating

With nightmarish dreams

Guilt-ridden and saddened

From their curses and screams

Shunning their family

Neighbor and friend

Knowing with others

Wounds they cause never mend

Alone and secluded

Is their preferred life to be

For crowds make them nervous

So to privacy they flee

Yes, these are our veterans

Some wounded in war

Who reside in the Psych Ward

In the VA's 8th floor

Thoughts and Reflections

PAIN

Pain and depression, they cut like a knife

And tears to the very heartbeat of life

They rip at the fabric of sanity and hope

And shreds peaceful living as it hangs by a rope

It carves out the joy that you once held so dear

And spits out the pieces both far and near

It grinds at the memories, erasing all dreams

Till the pain it brings forth explodes at the seams

It torments in nightmares, in the sounds all around

In the smells and the dust where it strives to be found

In reflections and flashes caught in the corner of eyes

The pain and depression fills our head full of lies

Paranoia then follows as swift as the wind

And our fears manifest till the night's bitter end

Then as we awaken with gasping for air

We struggle to realize the horrors aren't there

They're in the backs of our mind, they belong in the past

And we hope evermore that our symptoms won't last

We self-medicate with both liquor and drugs

Or ignore it completely sweeping it under the rug

We talk in our groups, or in therapy alone

Or when things turn real bad, then we pick up the phone   (cont)

Thoughts and Reflections

(cont)

We call to the hotlines, to the psychics, or docs

Hoping each we reach out to, finds the key that unlocks

To open the floodgates of gloom and despair

And release our burdens, set them free in the air

But alas the pain stays, though, forgotten at times

Till it ends up here as somebody's rhymes

So take all your pain, your depression and fears

And let me write of them, let me cry the tears

Let me be the voice of the pain that we share

Let me be the shoulder for the weight that you bear

Free up your burdens and smile once again

SO Sayeth our Savior, in His name....Amen.

Thoughts and Reflections

_____
_____
_____
_____
_____
_____
_____
_____
_____
_____
_____
_____
_____
_____
_____
_____
_____
_____
_____
_____
_____
_____
_____
_____
_____
_____
_____
_____
_____
_____
_____
_____
_____
_____
_____
_____

TO DREAM

To dream of peace instead of war,

Instead of nightmares frightening to the core

To dream of joy instead of hate,

Instead of heinous acts from evil innate

To dream of persons safe and sound

Instead of those whom misery has tied and bound

To finally rest when eyes are closed

Instead of the horror our world exposed

To finally sleep with peaceful thoughts

Instead of stomach wrenching knots

To finally wake with no regret

Not lying in a pool of sweat

To finally sleep and get some rest

Is what I dream, it's what I quest

And till that day of final peace

I pray each day the nightmares cease

Thoughts and Reflections

THE KNIGHT

My armor's on, my shield's in place

My demeanor is a stony face

My thoughts secure, my mask complete

My emotions hard as set concrete

My smile betraying the inner tears

Knowing no one now can see my fears

No one but me can see the pain

When persons ask without refrain

With questions wounding like arrows shot

About the past and battles fought

I would rather not talk or remember the past

I am crying inside while memories last

Yes, the "knight in shining armor" is here once again

Just please don't ask what I've done, where I've been

It brings up old memories I'd rather have hid

And my armor's the only things keeping a lid

On all the emotions, all of the pain

My helmet is faceless, it conceals once again

The hideous beasts called guilt and despair

Those dragons within me that none are aware,

Torment and fight me in this metal skin

Straining to burst free from this armor so thin

But they yield to me now as I learn how to cope

Which is giving me courage, and giving me hope

Thoughts and Reflections

SHADOWS

A shot rings out and I hit the floor

As shadows lurks behind each door

My eyes start racing to find the foe

With furtive glances for where to go

As I crawl around, I realize

I'm not where I have visualized

My mind sees things that are not there

Still preying on my deepest fear

The shot I heard…. Was just a car

But the shadows still as dark as tar

Thoughts and Reflections

REMINDERS

A weekly test of a tornado alarm

Makes me duck and hide from harm

A simple car horn takes me back

To places where I fear attack

A slamming door and fireworks

Takes me where the danger lurks

Outside myself, no danger near

But in my mind, I'm filled with fear

I look around and all I see

Are targets aiming back at me

I try to calm these aberrations

And that I'm not in those situations

I ground myself with three known facts

To remind me that I'm back, intact

And though this happens most every day

I still stand with pride each day and say

Though I've ventured places within my mind

A spark of sanity you'll find

That keeps me going and pressing on

Until the nightmares are said and gone

And though my fate's to relive the past

I'm still in control, the pain won't last

Thoughts and Reflections

THE HUMAN WITHIN

No matter the shine or dents in the steel

No matter the wounds that batter the will

No matter the armor that covers the skin

We must always remember the Human within

The Knight that comes saves us, or the Knight that we are,

Is never too distant, never too far

Always in armor, always feels safe

Always protected (though the armor must chafe)

But what of the human that hides in the shell?

The fragile frail body not doing so well?

They must wear the armor to hide all their doubt.

Confusion, and pain, fear within, and without

When may they then shed this metal tin suit?

When will the need for the armor be moot?

When is the battle for evil complete?

And the armor is shed, to fall at their feet?

When will we all get all along in this world?

When will attacks and rocks not be hurled?

It's only not needed, it will only be when,

We all can remember, the Human within.

Thoughts and Reflections

_____
_____
_____
_____
_____
_____
_____
_____
_____
_____
_____
_____
_____
_____
_____
_____
_____
_____
_____
_____
_____
_____
_____
_____
_____
_____
_____
_____
_____
_____
_____
_____
_____
_____
_____
_____
_____
_____
_____
_____

"ON"

Psychiatrists and counselors

Therapists and Peers

Seem to look on us as curs

Living off our fears

They see us when our depression's gone

And we're talking with a friend

Not realizing that our switch is "On"

And our smile is all pretend

We show our tee and twinkle eyes

In lobbies or waiting rooms

That's where the VA has their spies

Ready to drop the booms

They say "You're cured"

"We saw you laugh!"

Our denials then are spurned

From every VA staff

They don't know we have a switch

We turn daily "On" for friends

But in sessions and at home we twitch

And our depression never ends

(cont)

Thoughts and Reflections

_____
_____
_____
_____
_____
_____
_____
_____
_____
_____
_____
_____
_____
_____
_____
_____
_____
_____
_____
_____
_____
_____
_____
_____
_____
_____
_____
_____
_____
_____
_____
_____
_____
_____

We flip a switch so no one sees

The pain we really have

It's all an act for our friends to please

Kind of like a calming salve

We turn "On" so we don't flip

A switch that's deep within

That one will take us on a trip

Of where we've seen and been

We turn "On" and smile and wave

Shake hands with all we see

But deep inside in our dark cave

There lurks the enemy

It waits until our switch is "Off"ed

Till beaten down we lay

Exhausted by the smiles we doffed

Then attacks us as if we're a prey

It beats us down and wears us out

As we lay there in our beds

But that's not seen by those with "clout"

Who prescribe us all our meds

They only see that switch that's "On"

In our public face we show

Now realizing that our pain has gone

To a place we dare not go   (cont)

Thoughts and Reflections

(cont)

So don't believe our smile and grin

It's just a switch we flip

To avoid remembering we're we've been

Please don't take away our 'scrip!

Thoughts and Reflections

_____
_____
_____
_____
_____
_____
_____
_____
_____
_____
_____
_____
_____
_____
_____
_____
_____
_____
_____
_____
_____
_____
_____
_____
_____
_____
_____
_____
_____
_____
_____
_____
_____
_____
_____
_____

THE WAR CAME HOME

The War came home to me today

In a surreptitious, sneaky way

It came at me in a stealth attack,

While trapped I was flat on my back

It didn't arrive with a war decree

Or a declaration for all to see

It snuck into my home unheard

Without a hope of my mind to gird

Against the terror, the noise, the pain

For it nestled deep within my brain

It assaulted me when the house was dark

And brought the horrors in my mind to park

I didn't see or hear it come

Or tell the direction of where it's from

But seeping into my sleeping mind

It brough nightmares of the fiercest kind

The War now comes each time I sleep

And I pray the Lord my soul will keep

Me safe in His arms while I lay in bed

And fight these demons in my head

(cont)

Thoughts and Reflections

(cont)

And if the War comes home with you

I pray for you the same He'll do

We'll fight the War that haunts our sleep

And fight what demons come home to creep

Just as we survived that time away

We WILL Persist when War's home to stay

Thoughts and Reflections

STRUGGLES

My sorrows start with saddened sighs

Of failed attempts at suicides

I'll then regale you with my dreams

Of haunting things that cause my screams

My past forever deprived of hope

That led me to a hanging rope

I fought so hard to rid this curse

I thought was mine alone to nurse

But thanks to meds and therapy

My eyes were opened now to see

That though a past may haunt your soul

You're not a piece of a broken whole

You can be patched and put together

These harder times you'll learn to weather

With a future bright with friends, you'll see

You can fight this thing, P T S D

Thoughts and Reflections

POST-TRAUMATIC STRESS DISORDER

Cloudy skies within my head

With lightning striking nerves instead

That start fires of anger from all the pain

And I can't see thru the fog and rain

I can't think clear, the pain's intense

So I lash out with no pretense

No rationale, no thought control

My actions led by vitriol

I've tried so hard to be the kind

Of man who shows he owns his mind

That calmly walks in fearless manner

When danger strikes, I playful banter

I'd mock the hazards that came my way

But sadly now, I rue the day

For I jump at sounds, I leap at noises

My mind reacts without my choices

I've no control as I'd had before

The time I went across the shore

I went to where a nation called

But now of myself I've become appalled

(cont)

Thoughts and Reflections

_____
_____
_____
_____
_____
_____
_____
_____
_____
_____
_____
_____
_____
_____
_____
_____
_____
_____
_____
_____
_____
_____
_____
_____
_____
_____
_____
_____
_____
_____
_____
_____
_____
_____
_____
_____
_____
_____

(cont)

I take my meds, therapy and group

But so much of my life I can't recoup

Please know the storm within me now

Is not the me I will allow

I'll fight this storm with all my might

Till sunny skies are in my sight

Till the fog and rain have cleared my eyes

And peace and calm have been claimed the prize

I'll fight the storms that rages in

And try to blend in life again

Please be patient as I attempt to find

Methods proven to safe my mind

I try so hard to be as I was

For my life to live and my storms to pause

For someday soon, the storms shall avail

For the lightning to cease, the wrath, curtail

The anger ebbs like the tidal flow

The fog will clear, wherever fog my go

And to that day I work and pray

I take my pills as per VA

I go to class, I meditate

In hopes the storm will soon abate

My friends, don't worry, for I'm not a bomb

Ticking ever slowly till a spark like 'Nam   (cont)

Thoughts and Reflections

_____
_____
_____
_____
_____
_____
_____
_____
_____
_____
_____
_____
_____
_____
_____
_____
_____
_____
_____
_____
_____
_____
_____
_____
_____
_____
_____
_____
_____
_____
_____
_____
_____
_____
_____
_____
_____

(cont)

The Gulf, the Sands, an oilfield

Desert Storm or Desert Shield

Iraqi Freedom or World War II

OEF, and Mogadishu

Korea, The Big One, Grenada, yet you'll find

Even though these battles are all on our mind

We'll fight every day to battle the storm

That rage in our heads till finally the norm

Is to harness the weather and rein in the fury

That brings peace to all, and alleviates worry

And one day those clouds will soon dissipate

And the fog will soon lift, and my eyes will see straight

And to that day I beg of thee

Give time for me to be

Healing slowly as the storm did grow

Over time that I did not know

It built up slow, so now I ask

Be patient with me while I take to this task

Work with me, help me, pray if you can

Remember God made us, but we're still just human

Thoughts and Reflections

MY MIND IS MIA

In the deserts of my mind
In battles of the fiercest kind
There exists an awful fray
That fights within me every day

Within those crannies of my brain
Fulfilling tactics for which I've trained
Lies my thoughts, returning to
The war-torn sands of Timbuktu

Some far-off place I've never been
Or at least I can't remember when
But yet in my dreams I see so clear
Reflections of my deepest fear

Alone in battle, and alone in death
I gasp to take my dying breath
My body broken, my limbs all gone
As I expire with the morning dawn

The sun then rises, blinding eyes
And awaken me to ceiling skies
No longer lay I in desert air
But safe, secure, in reclining chair

(cont)

Thoughts and Reflections

(cont)

The dreams, they fade as fast as may

As I curse my mind that went MIA

For when my brain decides to go

It returns with scars I cannot show

A POW I then become

Trapped by dears and stricken numb

How I wish my thoughts would not travel so

And take me places I'd prefer not go

For my contract's over, I served with pride

I fought my battles, I dared not hide

Why then must my mind replay,

Fears that haunt me to this day?

Just this once I'd like to think my head

Would take me to a beach instead

Just my luck though, if and when it be

The beach would become my Normandy.

Thoughts and Reflections

PTSD

It's not clear why some have fear

And cracks appear in their demeanor

Making them sad, depressed and meaner

To all who try to help, and their burdens ease

Especially in times of hardship like these,

When fear drops them down hard on their very knees

As they stoically hold fast, and try to please

It's so hard for them when the grass is greener

And the "tough guys" heal quicker, cleaner

It's not clear why some have fear

Thoughts and Reflections

WHAT IS PTSD TO ME?

Dents in armor, cracks in steel

Holes in memories, kinks in the gears

Easily scared with many a fears

Paranoia strikes hard, pain feels very deep

Panic tendrils start within, slowly do they creep

While nerves are shot, and as wounds, slow they do seep

Sanity all lost from lack of sleep

Afraid of stigma, the looks, the leers

Afraid to be cast out from all your peers

Dents in armor, cracks in the steel

Thoughts and Reflections

A MOMENT IN TIME

Flash Frozen in the recess of my mind

Just a moment's flicker of fleeting time

An image snapped down deep into my soul

IN wrinkles, crevices, every hole

Grey matter shackled with imprinted fear

Paralyzing all that I hold so dear

My mind's eye can't unsee or blink away

The fateful thing that changed me on that day

It's not enough that I went thru Hell

I pray that there was just one I could tell

But till I can talk, silent I live life

With the fear I'll lose my kids and wife

Brooding, moody, angered, and shamed, I broke

From a moment in time, now it's my yoke

Thoughts and Reflections

HELMETS AND HARDSHIPS

In battles beaten, in harm's way hit

In tactics tested, in fights found fit

In trials tested tough and true

No better protection for our nations' few

The helmets' hardiness verified

From conflicts, skirmishes, it's sanctified

The brain beneath, so safe and sound

From all but for the deadliest round

The helmet worn by branches all

Of our nations' finest that heeded the call

They trust their lives to this Kevlar dome

Which in combat works to see them home

And once they're back and safe in bed

Then what, pray tell, protects their head?

What keeps their demons held at bay?

And keeps the dreams from out of the fray?

What hardships now must the vet endure,

To keep his thoughts and actions pure?

To stop from venting wrath untold,

From nightmares that every night unfold?

(cont)

Thoughts and Reflections

_____
_____
_____
_____
_____
_____
_____
_____
_____
_____
_____
_____
_____
_____
_____
_____
_____
_____
_____
_____
_____
_____
_____
_____
_____
_____
_____
_____
_____
_____
_____
_____
_____
_____
_____
_____
_____
_____

(cont)

To keep his loved ones closely by

When depression hits with pensive sigh

What hardships must this vet now face?

Now that life is at a slower pace?

There's no more action, the adrenaline's gone

From a shiny bright Knight to a lowly dim pawn

From an armored hero protecting the free

To unemployed now, with a disability

Would that the helmet was back to protect

The vet from those hardships, with all due respect

For PTSD takes its toll on a troop

And helmets can't help where the hardships regroup.

Thoughts and Reflections

MIDDLE AGE CRISIS

Strong I was, as any man

Till depression snuck in

With its own little plan

To defeat me where I couldn't win

I thought I could do it alone

Till the weight was too much to bear

And I found I had to pick up the phone

For someone my burdens to hear

What I once feared

Was what I didn't know

There were those that cared

When my feelings I'd show

There was someone who'd listen

There was someone to care

There was someone whose mission

Was my sorrows to share

I didn't know there are people around

To help for free and charging no cost

To life me when I'm feeling down

To find me when I'm utterly lost

(cont)

Thoughts and Reflections

(cont.)

There are text lines, call lines

Even support groups galore

There are people of all kinds

You just have to open that door

Don't let your sorry, your loneliness too

Your depression, your anger, and PTSD

Don't let them affect you, affect what you do

Seek someone now, you'll be thankful, like me.

Thoughts and Reflections

THE BOX OF PTSD

PTSD was a box I was in

Nestled deep and down within

Walls high and wide I couldn't climb

but things fell in and got in my mind

I didn't know because I couldn't see

the damage done outside of me

outside the box I pushed away

the very ones that I need to stay

The box kept filling with angst and stress

pressing its burden to excess

till one day the box and I both burst

it was, shamed to say, me at my worst

I finally saw as others did

when they'd look inside that cardboard lid

they'd see the anger, angst and fear

that I never saw while in trapped in there

I never knew I had a fault

From the times I'd led a troop assault

For there I was a leader of my men

And I couldn't break in front of them

(cont)

Thoughts and Reflections

(cont)

So stoically I came back home

not knowing I had a new syndrome

Traumatic Stress had built a box

protecting me from fear and shocks

It sheltered me but let me react

to things I imagined now were fact

I'd still see fights inside those walls

a cardboard copy of my downfalls

The scenes were only for me to see

inside the box that was holding me

but outside the wall it affected those

hurt as I lashed in violent throes

Reacting to sounds that didn't exist

but I heard in the box, or so I'd insist

Smells would drift in causing pain

and the box would be a desert again

But now the box, I've torn apart

its sides demolished, a fresh new start

I hope and pray a new box won't rise

so every day I pray to the skies

I work hard to calm my inner fights

to quell the dreams that haunt my nights   (cont)

Thoughts and Reflections

(cont.)

It takes an effort, it takes devotion

please understand, it's a deep ocean

For now, I struggle but I'm here to win

not trapped in a box like I was back then

Sink or Swim? No, I'm here to stay

If I can't swim, I'll just float today

I'll survive, and I 'll stay strong

Cause living in a box was wrong

Now free yourself if this rings true

Tear down those walls, don't let stress trap you.

Thoughts and Reflections

SILENT SUFFERING

Silent I stand, stoic and strong

Telling myself that I can go on

Fooling the ones with whom I converse

Playing so calm when in truth it's reverse

My anger is boiling, my angst oh so high

But calmly I stand there with barely a sigh

My outward appearance fools all but me

If only it was visible, my anxiety

I stress to the point of heartburn and pain

My head hurts, my chest aches, my eyes feel the strain

But I smile as you speak the words I abhor

And wait ever patient for you to exit the door

It's not until then that I let out a breath

That I had been holding like the skull of Macbeth

Alas, twas a friend that I knew oh so well

But holding it tightly caused my chest to swell

I sigh out with a loudness that even scares me

And wonder again if anyone could see

The fact that I stand there in Suffering Silence

To keep all my anger from erupting in violence

(cont)

Thoughts and Reflections

(cont.)

It's not that I'm hostile or a dangerous man

It's just that I've seen things I did not plan

I've gone thru more trauma than maybe you have

and my silence is band-aids, a patch or a salve

I invoke my right and the fifth I do plead

When the therapist states that my speech's what I need

to give an opinion and/or ascertain

the cause and the origin of all my pain

Silence is what keeps my life from corrupting

Any semblance of peace from my PTSD

It keeps the anger and pain from erupting

So please don't remove my Silence from me

Thoughts and Reflections

YOU HAVE NEVER

You've never heard my cry at night

You've never seen me weep

I spare you from the tragic sight

And hide while soft you sleep

You've never known how deep my fears

Affect the sleep I get

And you'll never get to dry my tears

Of that, I'll surely bet

You've never known I stay awake

Because I fear to sleep

And that someday my dreams will take

All that I wish to keep

I fear my hands will not be mine

Some night in wretched dreams

And try to take your life divine

While my mind sees violent scenes

No, you have known this side of me

With fear of nightmares coming true

And you have never known my agony

And I pray you never do

Thoughts and Reflections

WHAT WE NEED

Suicidal, homicidal, danger to all

That's what they call us, those that answered the call

They can't comprehend the dedication we serve

The guns and the fighting are all they observe

They don't understand, peace, our primary goal

Is that which we stand for deep down in our soul

We help oppressed persons, those needing a hand

We help them return to their homes and their land

We help those in need, we help those put out

We help to spread freedom in countries throughout

Our mission's not killing, our goal's to defend

Yet somehow there's those that can't comprehend

We come back from war, from combat and strife

And try to assimilate, to have a good life

But our mindset has changed, and not fort the good

Battling evil has made us so misunderstood

Now we're jumping at shadows with anxiety high

Not safe anymore, no matter how hard we try

(cont.)

Thoughts and Reflections

(cont.)

We see the threats out there, imagined or not

Our faith in humanity has been totally shot

Minds full of anguish, of battles intense

Or of suicide bombers from which there is no defense

But we're not really crazy like everyone thinks

We just need some time to smooth out all of those kinks

To adjust back to living in the land of the free

And somehow get a handle on our PTSD

So please don't consider us dangerous men

We just need some patience, we need …

A good friend

Thoughts and Reflections

DARK THOUGHTS

SUICIDE AWARENESS

Cold metal blade against my wrist

Goodbyes said to all on my list

Slicing slowly, the pain not felt

Just another agony Life to me has dealt

I've lost all hope, my dreams are gone

While people said to "just move on"

They've no idea how low I am

Nor did they offer to give a damn

If only someone had seen the signs

If only someone had heard my whines

If only someone had said to me

"There are other ways to set you free

There are places to go and people to call

From people who know what it's like to fall"

Yes, the helpline call could have saved my life

I realize now, as I lay down my knife

Had someone else recognized my pain

For I was just too low and no hope remained

So look my brothers to those in need

And talk to them before they do the deed

For they only know the depth and despair

And need just one person to say 'I care"

Thoughts and Reflections

FINAL REGRET

Futile thoughts as suicide beckons

Sadness overwhelming, darkness deepens

Pointless living, depression sinking

Pity on me the primary thinking

No remorse, no guilty feeling

Morbid thoughts make death appealing

No thoughts of loved ones, family, friend

One thought in mind, the goal, the End

My finger tightening, locked and loaded

A moment's flash, then all exploded

Now looking down, with regret I see

There were more important ones than me

Thoughts and Reflections

HELPLINE HOPE

In desperate tones I silently screamed,

For nightmares and death were all I dreamed

Behind my smiles my anguish reigned,

And I held it all in, as I'd been trained.

It ate my soul, me every thought

My every hope, my dreams all shot

A reason to live was all I needed

Before the sparks of hope had all receded

So I called the number with one last sigh

A helpline desk that I gave a try

And though moments away was I from death

I told them All in one big breath

They listened to me with such devotion

That despair became a fleeting notion

I still feel down, don't get me wrong

And my pain is there, it's never gone

But now I know there is someone to hear

Of the pain I have, of my despondent fear

There's always someone at the end of that line

To help find hope, and peace of mind

So call them please, when you spiral down

There's no better time, someone's _always_ around

Thoughts and Reflections

FINAL REMORSE

With one single action, I thought I'd be free

Now thinking back, it's with regret that I see

I was being selfish, so my thoughts would reflect

I didn't care whom my death would affect

I could not see my goal would only hurt others

And how my death would touch my sisters and brothers

If only I had talked or picked up the phone

And found there were more reasons than just me alone

More reasons to march on, more reasons to live

To boldly go on with my one life to live

My one life so it seems would affect so much more

Than just ending my suffering and closing that door

There are people who know me and people that care

And those to whom my passing would be totally unfair

My life's but a strand of a web so complex

That I never realized the number it affects

I now know the suffering that would have ended that day

Would cause so much more grief than any could say

My family and friends would all wonder why

And be torn all apart by my sudden goodbye

(Cont)

Thoughts and Reflections

(cont.)

So with all due remorse to my most selfish of thought

I live proudly knowing that I caused no distraught

Yes, my pain is intense and my suffering is real

But surviving is the first step to beginning to heal

So reach out to someone if you are considering

        The Deed

And remember those loved one... and to healing

        GODSPEED

Thoughts and Reflections

_____
_____
_____
_____
_____
_____
_____
_____
_____
_____
_____
_____
_____
_____
_____
_____
_____
_____
_____
_____
_____
_____
_____
_____
_____
_____
_____
_____
_____
_____
_____
_____
_____
_____
_____
_____
_____

SUICIDE HOTLINE POEM

In desperate times I've held the rope

In darkness black when I couldn't cope

In deep low places I've pulled the hammer

When despair and grief in silence clamor

When despondency brought me to the blade

And depression its final argument made

When all hope was lost and gave in I did

To the Final Deed which all forbid

Yet before the act a voice rang clear

Which reminded me about my fear

That it's not my life I would be taking

But the lives of loved ones I'd be forsaking

My pain would end but theirs would start

And I would leave them all with broken heart

No reason given, I'd just be gone

And do to them the greatest wrong

So yet in darkness then there still was light

For which I struggled hard and fought the fight

I pulled myself up and found you can survive

By calling 1 800 273 8255

Thoughts and Reflections

STOP ME

Wondering

Thinking out loud if I can

Why is it my life that's sinking

Is it some cosmic plan?

The depths that I'm dwelling

Seem to be to no end

And my protests and yelling

Bring no one to mend

I feel that there's no one

That understands my sorrow

And I doubt I'll see Sun

By this time tomorrow

All I need is a person

A relative or friend

To rid this here toxin

And my depression upend

I know that can't cure me

Or stop my mind if it's set

But I know they'll assure me

Suicide's not my kismet

(cont)

Thoughts and Reflections

(cont)

Just one little soul

One person I pray

Please stop my goal

Put my plan at bay

I don't care about who

Please help change my mind

Maybe it's you

Just someone, be kind

You just never know

Whose depression, they hide

And their darkness won't show

But they're right by your side

So smile today and make you a friend

For you never can say whose plan you might end

For if only you'd smile, perhaps just a wave

It might take a while, but a life, you might save!

Thoughts and Reflections

SADNESS

Fuzzy grayness fills my soul

As darkened thoughts surround me

Depression takes a heavy toll

As heart beats ever slowly

Tears flow free as pain erupts

From within my core so deep

As if my insides rip my guts

And blood from the wound does seep

Clouds grow dark in skies above

As gloom and doom defeat me

For pain so great has come from love

Which left me sad and lonely

For once true love has touched your heart

Then leaves so quick and harshly

The anguish shreds your world apart

And heartbreak tears completely

Thoughts and Reflections

741-741

When life has you handing

By a fragile thin thread

And you hear creditors banging

As you lay in your bed

The phone won't stop ringing

With late notice calls

At the door, dogs are barking

While echoes bounce down the halls

Stress has your hands wringing

Holding covers over your head

And life has no meaning

But death does instead

With tasks overwhelming

Please pick up your phone

There's a number for texting

Your state of your home

Then send the words to the number, 741-741

And wait for the call, that's all needs to be done

Here's hoping the caller

Can help with your pain

And I pray that your future

Is bright once again

Thoughts and Reflections

MY PAST

I left it all, I left my house

Walked right out on my kids and my spouse

I ran with the thought to finish it all

From too much stress, from too far a fall

I thought their lives would be better off

If I wasn't there for them to scoff

I thought my death would bring them life

Instead of dragging down my kids and wife

I looked for ways to do the deed

Like cut my wrists, then lie and bleed

Or jump in front of a moving truck

But no semis drove by, just my luck

Suicide by cop seemed an easy pick

But as I approached the car, he left really quick

He'd never know the guilt my death would have given

But another call had let me stay with the living

I pondered hanging from a tall, tall tree

But the climbing thing I just couldn't see

I wanted another to do the crime

To put me into my peace sublime

(cont)

Thoughts and Reflections

(cont)

A coward I was, or so I thought

I just couldn't be the one to take the shot

I broke down again, from fear of dying

Yet thoughts of death would ease my crying

I felt that no one understood

Why I'd want to end my life for good

It was logic and plain easy for me to see

But others couldn't, and wouldn't, let it be

They counsel, coerce, console, and cry

When I just felt it was my time to die

Yet somehow amidst all my trouble and strife

I learned to value this thing called life

It took a few visits of in-patient sessions

Of intensive therapy, pills, medications

It took realizing that though I've seen much

My mind and body were just out of touch

I learned that my life is not mine to take

That I need to live for all my loved ones' sake

My parents, my children, my spouse all would hurt

As they lowered me down and threw handfuls of dirt

(cont)

Thoughts and Reflections

(cont)

The flag would be folded and handed down with respect

As my family, my friends, would on my life then reflect

They'd remember my fondly though with sadness and grief

Shaking their heads in morose disbelief

Yes, my passing would create to them so much pain

By the fact that my dying would bring nothing to gain

Don't get me wrong not, I've thought it all through

And I'm going to live- for me, them, and you.

Thoughts and Reflections

UNASHAMED

Since those days I tried to hide

My fateful days of suicide

I thought that folks would mock me so

Because of times I tried to go

As I look back, I've learned to say

Depression clenched my soul at bay

It held me in its tightest grip

And there my mind began to slip

It wasn't logic in the simplest terms

That led my mind to feed the worms

With the dead corpse, I'd finally have a cause

I'd end my life without so much a pause

But treatment came in many a form

From pills and counselors to make me "norm"

I'm still not cured, my mind still haunts

Those deep dark places with those chilling taunts

But I've learned how now to control desire

To dance to close to the "suicide fire"

Like a moth to flame I fight to live

Every bit of strength this fight I give

(cont)

Thoughts and Reflections

_____
_____
_____
_____
_____
_____
_____
_____
_____
_____
_____
_____
_____
_____
_____
_____
_____
_____
_____
_____
_____
_____
_____
_____
_____
_____
_____
_____
_____
_____
_____
_____
_____
_____
_____
_____

(cont)

I stand now proud that I've survived

The attempts, the thoughts, the times I tried

I'm here to tell you, you're not alone

When depression hits, just pick up the phone

There are people to talk to, text or write

That are there to help you in this struggle, this fight

People who've been there, people that know

What "checking out" means, when you feel it's your time to go

The most meaningful thing is that you swallow your pride

Don't be ashamed, don't cower, don't hide

Talk to someone, bend their ear, make them hear

Make them listen to you, let them know what you fear

Be unashamed of asking for aid

And talk to someone till the urges they fade

Never let pride ever stand in your way

Of seeking some help to live one more day

So be unashamed, we all have our lows

Be unashamed, sometimes that's how life goes

Be unashamed, for to lives what you seek

Be unashamed, no more are you weak

(cont)

Thoughts and Reflections

(cont)

Be unashamed, that you once fell so deep

As to drift in that darkness of eternal sleep

So you once fell, but you are up once again

And be unashamed, for He's forgiven your sin

Be unashamed, tell the world that you live

And be unashamed, for some peace you may give

To a soul that is aching, a soul torn apart

A soul ripped asunder, a fresh broken heart

You survived to live on, and I did as well

To tell all the world that it's not worth the Hell

It's not worth the torment, the anguish, the pain

That your loved ones will feel when your memory's slain

For life is worth living, if not for them, then for you

Just keep on with hoping and making your life all anew

Keep on believing there are things you don't know

But first be unashamed, and your courage will grow.

You see, I'm not ashamed, I cried out and got aid

When suicide seemed the only way, I was afraid

But I got some help, you can too if you try

So be Unashamed, you're not weak if you cry

Thoughts and Reflections

AWASH ON THE SHORE

Alone on the beach

Of depression, despair

The waves out of reach

In the cold, wintry air

Whitecaps just taunting

And teasing of hope

With larger waves daunting

Like the end of your rope

Sands shifting silent

As your thoughts while you walk

Got to sad, dark and violent

And an outline of chalk

But who'd find the remains

Of the way that you've planned?

And who'd be there to explain

Of a corpse in the sand?

Who'd know the cause,

The rhyme or the r3easons

You gave your life pause

In this cold weather season?

(cont)

Thoughts and Reflections

But as you ponder these questions,

There's light on the shore

That breaks ruminations

As from a lighthouse it pours

The light, it surrounds you

And warms to your soul

Breaking up despair blue

That has taken its toll

You feel now there's hope

From the beacon so bright

That now you can cope

As you bathe in its light

Then dawn slowly breaks

And the dark fades away

As the sunrise it takes

All your blues on this day

So let the light find you

Whenever life's bland

Let waves of hope crash through

Your line in the sand

Let your light shine

From within and without

And know you'll be fine

Of that never doubt

Thoughts and Reflections

I THINK I WOKE UP DEAD TODAY

I think I woke up Dead Today

But I'm not really sure

I think I woke up Dead Today

But I was looking for a cure

To end my pain and suffering

To cease the guilt and shame

I thought all that was ending

And there'd be no more to blame

I think I woke up Dead Today

I was hoping not to live

I think I woke up Dead Today

For I had nothing left to give

But no, I woke up seeing light

Bright and shining in my eyes

In a metal bed that held me tight

With straps of leather and ties

The light, I hoped was Heaven's beam

But I regret that wasn't so

So then the straps in my mind, they seemed

To be chains from Down Below

(cont)

Thoughts and Reflections

I think I woke up Dead Today

If only someone had listened

I think I woke up Dead Today

But that's not what I had destined

I think I woke up Dead Today

And I screamed to no avail

I think I woke up Dead Today

From my nights of living Hell

Instead I woke in hope, and pain

Still found among the living

And I must say I won't try that again

For Death is not forgiving

I think I woke up Dead Today

His grasp was ever fleeting

I think I woke up Dead Today

So GLAD my heart's still beating

So GLAD I woke ALIVE today

For I learned Death's not the answer

So GLAD I woke ALIVE today

For Depression's like a cancer

It can be fought, - I'm learning how

And to myself I must be true

I'm so glad I'm in the here and now

And I hope that you are too!

Thoughts and Reflections

EVEN ROCKS CRUMBLE

Granite hard and stony faced

I've lived my life as I 've been placed

A stoic person, head held high

With marbled glaze in steely eye

Always there to bear the weight

Of the burdens that have become my fate

To stand with shoulders squared away

Like bedrock firm in a stalwart way

Entrenched so others do not fail

Alongside me, their strength prevails

I give them hope, support, and aid

So through life's hardships they can wade

But even now my veneer has cracked

My very core, less than intact

From pressures too intense to bear

As I forgot my own self care

I let self-doubt and worry in

And contemplated the unforgiving Sin

My strength for others had taken a tumble

For I learned the hard way, even hard rocks crumble

(cont)

Thoughts and Reflections

(cont.)

So learn this lesson, as I relate to you

Stand strong, be strong, to thine own self be true

Take care of yourself, your mind, your all

And don't be discouraged, because sometimes, ...

Rocks fall

Thoughts and Reflections

DEPRESSION: ALONE IN THE DARKNESS

Alone in the Darkness, so foreboding

Heartbeat nags, as if it's goading

With every thump to end its beating

While silence pounds till ears are bleeding

Yet in this cave that's been created

Cries for help somehow abated

Echoes return with mantras shouted

And all complaints are firmly doubted

Tears, they fall, as stalagmites, rise

Upon the floor till their very size

Imprison me within the very stone

Of a little Hell I call my Own

Yet somehow, I struggle thru the day

This cave I carry in some morbid way

For within my mind this cave ensnares

My very soul, my joy, my cares

Thoughts and Reflections

HOPE AND FAITH

H.O.P.E

When pain persists and rips away

Your sanity, your will to stay

When it strips the core of what you are

And it's taken you past the edge too far

Remember pain is just a thing

To remind you there is more to gain

Healing comes to those who wait

Who take the pain along with fate

For wounds will close, scars will fade

Help will come from friends you've made

Remember the letters h. o. p. e.

Spell them out, and you will see

They stand for what I promise you, friends

Always remember, Hang On, Pain Ends

Thoughts and Reflections

HEALING HAS NO TIME LIMIT

They say that time will heal all wounds

Well of course that's understood

When time is like the endless dunes

Of the Saharas of our Hollywood

Healing has no limit to

How short or long it takes

Nor will it ever give a clue

To the recovery of your aches

For wounds of heart and soul are deep

They've cut you to the core

They're not just bruise or scratch that seep

But a festering open sore

The heart bleeds pain and aches immense

There's no equivalent

It's torture, for in common sense,

It's suffering, true lament

But keep the faith that time will heal

Just don't hold it to a clock

And you'll soon find the scars congeal

And all Life and Love you'll GROK!!!!

Thoughts and Reflections

INSIDE

I've spent some time inside those walls

that house the screams, the cries, the calls

the pleas for help, from terrors heard

from within our mind, the voices blurred

I've spent some time inside you see

to earn the title "ill, mentally"

Depression, post-traumatic stress disorder

was my norm, it gave no quarter

It filled my head with thoughts so grave

it was a wonder they my life could save

I tried to take my life so oft

at Death I thumbed my nose to scoff

I thought that Death was the only way

but now I live each day to say

No matter the darkness, no matter the pain

You've so much life and joy to gain

And if you go inside those walls

for the Thorazine shuffle down the halls

Remember it's only a time to heal

To gather thoughts, to hope and feel

For time inside is not for shame,

for embarrassment, or public pain

It's time to get things right, anew

and if you go Inside, I'm there for you!

Thoughts and Reflections

DON'T STOP DREAMING

When terror strikes deep in your mind

with horrors of the fiercest kind

when frightening images grip your soul

and night sweats take a ravaging toll

when panic takes your very breath

you swear you'd welcome a timely death

Please don't let the nightmares win

that often crush the strongest men

Dig deep inside yourself, your heart

with each night must be a brand-new start

lay your head and gently sleep

and if the nightmares come back to creep

inside your thoughts, invade your peace

remember this to make them cease

though you wake in fitful screaming

You've must remember, don't stop dreaming

nightmares are only the worst of thought

from anxious times, a caveat

a way to keep you from hope and pride

to keep your true thoughts deep inside

so let them out, your goals, desires

Don't stop dreaming, keep lighting those fires

Their light will slowly burn the fear

that infests your mind, till the ashes clear

Don't stop dreaming, never give in

Sleep my friend, it's time again

Thoughts and Reflections

BRING IT

Restless Demons full of fight

Torment me thru endless night

Spirits' screams are incoherent

Their purpose though is so apparent

Walking hours filled with fear

Distrust to all whom dared to near

Paranoia rears its ugly head

Replacing hope with doubt and dread

I did not ask this for my life

To be wounded sharp by pain and strife

But I'd gladly bear the brunt of all

And proudly suffer standing tall

For my life was serving others first

So bring pain on and do your worst

You'll find though broken I will emerge

With nervous tension on the verge

I'll bear the scars as best I can

And with honor shining here I stand

Before you now I humbly try

To look you squarely in the eye

(cont.)

Thoughts and Reflections

(cont.)

To tell you I, though tattered, torn

Will not mock you, will not scorn

I, too, feel pain, I feel the hurt

From playing in the "sand box" dirt

And gladly do it all again

With pain my partner, fear my friend

To rise each morning with pride and say,

I'm here for you, and I'm here to stay

Thoughts and Reflections

REDEMPTION

Bars of Iron, Commode of Steel

All designed to break ones' will

Orange jumpsuits just in case

Easy to spot when they give chase

Little cell about 5 by 7

So no mistaking that for Heaven

A piece of Hell just for the sins

When Luck runs out and Justice wins

Laws were broken as is the spirit is now

"Never sin again". A most solemn vow

Sounds, they echo throughout the halls

As Time ticks slower when inside those walls

Was Fate the cause, or bad decisions?

As skillful guilt makes sharp incisions

That cuts ones' pride, one's will to live

As Hope is slashed, with nothing more to give

But once the time inside is done

And by best behavior a few years won

Released to smell fresh air again

But still marked a felon from your sin

(cont.)

Thoughts and Reflections

(cont.)

No chance to vote, nor own a gun

Nor find a job as day is done

The hardest part for the crime you did

Is keeping details of life well hid

But remember there's One two whom you're free

For He died for your sins on a tall, wood tree

He forgave your sins, your violent ways

So that all you need do, is sing His praise

He's waiting to enter that cold, vile heart

And from His bosom, no, you'll never part

You may go astray, but once He's in

Just ask forgiveness for all your sin

Confess your wrongs, repent your ways

And you'll be at peace thru all your days

Your time you spent behind the cage

Is another past chapter, another past page

Another past life before God came in

And Jesus cleansed you of all your sin

So bring your worries to the altar and pray

And let God again, in your heart, forever to stay

Thoughts and Reflections

MORE LIFE TO LIVE

I got to a point I'd given thought

Of giving up, of saying "why not?"

But then a light dawned ever bright

A small, still voice showed me the light

It gave me hope when all was lost

When I'd almost paid the final cost

When I almost pulled the trigger back

When I'd almost taken the long dark track

So much for thinking that life had to end

That all was a needless, wasteful trend

And for wanting my world to finally crash

And to just heap my body upon the trash

I've found that life isn't done by far

There's so much more to this shining star

It's burning bright, this ball of fire

The flame forever, higher and higher

So much more there is to find

So much more to expand my mind

So much more life has to give

So much life there is to live

(cont.)

Thoughts and Reflections

(cont.)

It's not time to quench or snuff the flame

I'll not let Darkness to my Life lay claim

I'll fight the shadows, the mists of doubt

To ensure my candle is not blown out

There's so much more to live, to love

So many gifts from Heaven above

I have so much Life to Live it's clear

I'm hanging on for many a year

I'll not give up, I'll not give in

For that would be the greatest sin

When there's so much life worth living for

More Life to Live is what I implore

Continue living each day, my friend

As if on a journey that will never end

Like scooping oceans in a sieve

There's so much more of Life to Live

Please keep on, no matter what

Stay Safe, stay strong, don't get in a rut

Keep hope and faith alive, my friends,

Remember H.O.P.E. , Hang On , Pain Ends

Thoughts and Reflections

HOW WILL I CLIMB THIS?

How am I going to climb this

Mountain in front of me?

How am I going to find the bliss,

Of a goal I cannot see?

How will I ever find the peak

Or reach the apogee?

When all is daunting, all looks bleak

Of this climb in front of me

How am I going to find my path,

That lies before me now?

I've crunched the numbers, done the math

It eludes me all somehow

But then, the air above the hill

Shines with rays so bright

The Sun brings hope to find the will

To press forward with my plight

The warmth of dawn from beyond my goal

Reminds me of my mother

Who, more than once, God rest her soul

Said, "Just put one foot in front of the other!"

(cont.)

Thoughts and Reflections

(cont.)

And so, I'll climb this arduous mount

One step at a time

I'll make this journey, on that you can count

That's how I'll make this climb!

Thoughts and Reflections

FIND THE BLESSING

Find the Blessing in your curse

Just tell yourself, it could be worse

There is always something down the road

Harder, rougher, a heavier load

Look for the silver around your cloud

The lining's there, all safe and sound

It's tucked away for you to find

It's just a matter of using your mind

To see the brightness thru the haze

Don't let your doubts put out your blaze

See the lightning withing the storm

As power, and energy, above the norm

Use it, harness it, control its flow

Tap that source to make yours glow

Find the benefit, not the harm

And live your life blessed by the charm

The power is yours, and yours alone

It's a skill to learn, a skill to hone

But I have faith that your will find

Your Curse a Blessing to be redefined

(cont.)

Thoughts and Reflections

(cont.)

Keep believing that all turmoil

Can turn the fiercest soldier loyal

The bravest warriors come from war

And Heroes come from battles galore

They're the Blessings from horrific times

That save our lives, prevent the crimes

From with the Curses of Life's own making

Find the Blessings your undertaking

Give it all you have to find the Best

Stay Positive my friend, Stay Well, Stay Blessed

Thoughts and Reflections

CHOOSE OR BLUES

I sit in my reclining chair,

reflecting on the words to share

I want everyone to be aware,

There's hope and promise in the air

The masses try to sit and pout

of all the things they've done without.

They grumble, whine, spit and spout

complaints and cuss the whole day out.

But I'm here to tell you this my friend

This, like all things, will someday end.

It may not happen just round the bend

but soon we'll see the downward trend.

And through it all we have to Choose

an attitude of hope or blues.

For though I listen to all the news

I know the doomsday scare's a ruse

I must keep my hopes and dreams alive

and choose my life is going to thrive

I'll stay attentive, as threats arrive

but my positive thoughts this won't deprive

It won't take my joy, my very soul

and thrust it in some deep dark hole

Affirm yourselves, stick to this role

Choose Life my friends, make it your goal

Thoughts and Reflections

WEAR IT BOLDLY

Take pride in troubles you've survived

Take pride in wounds that scarred your hide

Take pride in conflicts you've been through

And all the hardships done to you

Take pride I say, don't feel ashamed

Take pride, you're aren't the one to blame

Take pride in how you now react,

Now use compassion and use your tact

The trials you've been through have made you stronger

Especially when you felt you could hold on no longer

Things you've experienced, things you've seen

Are actually a gift, made you wiser, made you keen

Your experiences allow you to see beyond

What could have been, what could go on

Take pride that you have lived your life

Thru all the hardships, all the strife

Wear your badge of honor well

Stick out your chest and make it swell

Beam with pride you made this far

Don't let your past shoot down your star

(cont.)

Thoughts and Reflections

(cont.)

Take pride and wear your history bold

Show others that you aren't ice cold

The fires you've walked through made you heal

And forged a weapon made of steel

This tool created helps you fight

What troubles you, whatever blight

So shine with strength and carry through

Wear with pride this thing called YOU!!

Thoughts and Reflections

ONLY HAVE UP TO GO

When life's the lowest and things look grim

When shadows fall and lights go dim

When heartache, suffering have you down

When sadness brings your face to frown

When rock bottom's hit with landing hard

When the hand you're dealt is short a card

When the gutter is where you lay your head

When guardian angels have up and fled

When hope and dreams are up in smoke

When the albatross becomes your yoke

When suicide seems all that's left

When all the joy in life's bereft

When you've reached this point this you must know

It's now you only have UP to go

There's only UP, one place remains

No more to lose, there's only gains

Find hope, find peace in knowing this

UP is where to find your Bliss

So start the ladder at the bottommost rung

Climb out of the muck, the mire, the dung

Remember UP to reach the sky

For Life's always worth another try

Take each step up and know my friend

I'll be there for you, till the very end

Thoughts and Reflections

ROCKS IN MY PATH

My journey was halted the other day

By a huge boulder in my way

It looked ancient to behold

It blocked my path and stopped me cold

This rock my progress would interfere

So I gave in to sadness, gave in to fear

I began to think of suicide

I prayed, I wept, oh how I cried

But then my tears which flowed like rain

Formed two rivers from all the pain

I watched two rivers merge to one

And under the boulder slowly run

It formed a gorge, a canyon large

The rock began to soon discharge

Eroded by the tears I shed

Moved by sorrow's riverbed

Slow my path once more revealed

My life the boulder had just concealed

I watched the rock just float on by

Easing self-pity, stopping my cry

(cont.)

Thoughts and Reflections

(cont.)

I reflected no matter what stands in my way

Rocks are just things, not obstructions per se

They may cause stumbling or stubbing a toe

Temporarily blocking or making you slow

Remember this, rocks on your road

Crumble in nature, and soon erode

Rivers fed by tears of sorrow

Give way to brighter days tomorrow

A Rock, a boulder, along your life

Is just a thing, not cause for strife

Climb over, go 'round, or just push through

And know my friend, I'm there for you.

Thoughts and Reflections

RESOURCE PAGE

EMERGENCY CONTACT NUMBERS

National Suicide Prevention Hotline - 800-273-8255 (TALK)

Colorado Crisis Services 1-844-493-8255 (TALK)

Trevor Lifeline for LGBTQ 1-866-488-7386

First Responder Hotline 1-844-550-4376 (HERO)

National Alliance on Mental Illness: 1-800-950-6264

National Domestic Violence Hotline 1-800-799-7233

National DEAF Domestic Violence Hotline 1-855-812-1001

Rape, Abuse and Incest National Network 1-800-656-4673

National Child Abuse Hotline 1-800-422-4453 (4ACHILD)

TEXT HOTLINE

TEXT 'HELP' TO 741-741

TWITTER
@800273TALK

NEW NATIONAL THREE DIGIT SUICIDE HOTLINE NUMBER 988

BIOGRAPHY

Steven Bates

Steven Bates turns 56 in May 2022.

Steven is a veteran of the Air Force Reserves and active Air Force, serving for a combined total of eighteen years before being medically discharged in 2003. He has also served his civilian community prior to active duty as a Police officer and Corrections officer in Panama City, Fla.

Since leaving the military, Steven tried working as an Assistant Manager for a truck stop and as a city level Water Department Dispatcher but sadly his physical and mental disabilities prevented the consistency and capabilities needed to remain steadily and gainfully employed.

After five failed suicide attempts and a few voluntary stays in treatment facilities he turned back to poetry as a way of coping, having always used poetry in the past for dealing with just about everything life had thrown at him.

Steven started writing books and volunteering his time as a suicide attempt survivor support facilitator, using his unique past experiences and poetry for suicide prevention after it was revealed to him that a set of poems that he had written for a suicide prevention month program actually prevented a suicide from happening. This was the catalyst for Poemspeak.org and has changed his entire focus from the desire to be a famous poet to now being someone who helps others through poetry.

Steven now lives in Alabama with his wife and two dogs. He spends his time writing poetry, organizing local gaming events, playing video games, and learning each day how to make the best from living with fibromyalgia, PTSD, depression, arthritis, COPD, two brand new knees.

His latest poetry can be viewed freely at www.facebook.com/stevenbatesmusings/ and he can be reached thru Facebook, thru the Poemspeak website, or thru Twitter @stevenbatespoet.

Made in the USA
Columbia, SC
23 December 2022

73903665R00115